THAILAND

TIGER BOOKS INTERNATIONAL

Text
Steve Van Beek

Graphic design
Patrizia Balocco

Map
Arabella Lazzarin

Contents

1 *Mae Toranee, the mythical goddess who wrung rivers of water from her hair to drown the demons disturbing the meditating Buddha as he reached Enlightenment, stands near Sanam Luang Park.*

2-3 *The crown jewel of Thai Buddhism, Wat Phra Kaew (the Temple of the Emerald Buddha), with the triple-spired Grand Palace behind it, is the spiritual heart of Thailand. Its architecture is a metaphor for everything Thai: warm colours, a human dimension, the chaos of the jungle compressed into a courtyard, and a multiplicity of contrasting styles which somehow blend as if fused together by a molten tropical sun. The Royal Chapel, the hall on the left, shelters the Emerald Buddha, a small jadeite image with a history as turbulent as that of early Thailand.*

4-5 *Gold is the element of homage, the ultimate demonstration of one's piety. It clads all religious objects, and many which are not, including this bronze mythical kinaree. It is one of eight silent guardians which ring the Prasat Phra Thepidon, the Royal Pantheon. A core building in Wat Phra Kaew, the Pantheon contains statues of the first eight kings of the present dynasty.*

6 *Lotus flowers lift their heads above a monastery pond. Because it rises from the muck of swamps, the lotus symbolizes the purity of Buddha's teachings in an unclean world.*

7 *Each morning, village women in their volcano hats paddle quietly to the Floating Market to sell farm produce and meals created in their kitchens in pre-dawn hours.*

10-11 *Evening on the Kok River, a minor northern stream which flows from the small town of Tha Thon through the metropolis of Chiang Rai and on to the Mekong River.*

12-13 *Red-ruffed women of the Yao hilltribe in the far north excel in embroidering intricate patterns on their turbans and clothes.*

14-15 *Each March, when the winds from the south struggle to blow away the heat of the hot season, the blue heavens are dotted with patches of colours as children of all ages launch colourful kites. Sanam Luang, adjacent to Wat Phra Kaew, is a favoured kite-flying site.*

This edition published in 1994 by TIGER BOOKS INTERNATIONAL PLC , 26a York Street Twickenham TW1 3LJ, England.

First published by Edizioni White Star. Title of the original edition: Thailandia, il regno dei templi d'oro. © World copyright 1994 by Edizioni White Star, Via Candido Sassone 22/24, 13100 Vercelli, Italy.

ISBN 1-85501-477-7

Printed in Singapore by Tien Wah Press Color separations by Magenta, Lit. Con., Singapore.

Interior of the temple of
Wat Nang Chi in Bangkok.

Sailing along the Wang River.

The gold-plated steeple of the temple of
Wat Phra Keo in Bangkok.

Introduction

Colour and chaos are the twinned elements of the vibrant rice bowl nation once called Siam, and now known as Thailand. A tropical kingdom the size of France, its borders embrace a melange of cultural homogeneity and surprising geographical diversity that for centuries has enticed travellers on east-west passages through the Orient.

The character of its natural beauty provides a key to understanding the people who inhabit it. Powdery sand beaches rimming the Gulf of Thailand and the Andaman Sea, divide azure ocean reefs from jade green jungles. The low shore is lapped by low waves, its benign nature providing a good introduction to the lifestyles pursued in the interior of the country. Moving inland, the blue waves lapping the shores meld into green waves of rice lapping at forested mountains. Silver rivers and thousands of miles of natural and man-made canals flow down these mountains and provide the sustenance the rice-rich valleys require.

Thailand is traditionally divided into four regions. The Central Plains, with the royal capital of Bangkok, is the heartland of the nation. It is the kingdom's most prosperous area, comprising a broad valley carpeted in rice and vegetables - a garden hemmed on the west by the Tenassirim Range that forms the border with Burma. On the east, the valley floor rises to the Khorat Plateau. The Plateau is the dominant feature of the second region, the Northeast, which ends at the flowing waters of the Mekong River delineating the border with Laos; its southeastern border is shared with Cambodia. Thailand's poorest region, the Northeast, is a treeless expanse whose wealth lies in its ancient architecture and spirited folk culture. Dangling like an oxtail from the western portion of the Central Plains is a narrow peninsula that broadens as it drops south towards the equator, crossing the border into Malaysia and then, Singapore. Know simply as "The South", its economy and Muslim-based culture distinguishes it from the rest of Buddhist Thailand. Here, minarets stand like watchtowers above rubber and coconut plantations which vie with tin mines as the region's principal income earners.

The country's most varied scenery is found in the North along the borders with Laos and Burma. Its location at the far eastern end of the Himalayas has made it a land of peaks and valleys in varying hues of green. Until 1938, *Lanna* ("Land of a Million Rice Fields"), as it is known, was an autonomous kingdom. Its remoteness from Central Plains'

influences enabled it to blend the two distinct cultures of its neighbours with its own perceptions to create a unique culture reflected in thousands of beautiful temples and art objects. Its principal city, Chiang Mai, is regarded as the country's cultural capital and in its back streets can be found the workshops which produce the lacquerware, silver jewellery, bronze images, wood carvings and ceramics for which *Lanna* is famed.

Thailand is essentially an agricultural nation, making green its predominant colour. Colour accents are found in the Buddhist temples which dot the countryside and provide spiritual and visual oases in the towns. They are also found in clothing, in folk pageantry, and the hues with which Thais embellish even the most mundane utensils. This penchant for bright pigments would be expected in a tropical country whose jungles hold brilliantly-coloured flowers, birds, and butterflies, but here it is treated with an exuberance which creates visual excitement and suggests the vitality of its people.

The swirl of colour is also representative of the chaos that surrounds one. The tangled confusion of the jungle has been replicated in the design (or lack of it) of towns and urban homes. Few towns are marked by grids, streets names (some bearing four different names along their lengths) or consecutive house numbering, and few are divided into distinct administrative, commercial, or residential districts.

This casual approach to town planning reflects Thais' general distaste for dogma and contributes much to their charm. Although they work long hours, Thais take a serene view of life. Strangers meet and are friends for life, an outsider is invited to share a meal as a prelude to a friendship; smiles and easy laughter are evident everywhere. Even in busy Bangkok, an office visit is highlighted by an offer of coffee and a leisurely half hour of relaxed conversation on a wide range of topics, few of them related to business.

The chaos is also reflected in a dynamism evident from the wet markets to office suites, an energy which has transformed much of the country's geographic and economic landscape over the past decade. The incongruity is that amidst the chaos -and, in the cities, the cacophony - the Thais themselves display a detached tranquillity and a calmness of bearing. Crushed together, they tolerate others and are willing to share limited space. This unity of purpose and temperament amidst the confusion makes them unique among Asian nations in never having fought a religious or civil war. Contrasting cultures live side by side in harmony, sharing common responses to problems that affect them all, and overlooking their differences. It is this warmth and unanimity that gives the country its strength and makes the people its principal assets.

The face that Bangkok presents to the world is like that of the demon king *Tosakan* in the culture's most famous "khon" (masked) drama, the *Ramakhien*. The mask is by turns majestically

16 *A miniature replica of the Anandakaviloka, one of the principal Royal Barges, is displayed at a celebration in Sukhothai, Thailand's capital from 1238 to 1350. Although a creation of the succeeding Ayutthayan period (1350-1767), the barge blends well with the serene, Sri Lankan-inspired spires of the ancient city.*

terrifying and repellingly ugly. Behind the mask, however, is a human face, warm, spirited, and so welcoming that makes one forget the grotesqueness of the varnished veneer that hides it.

So, too, with Bangkok. Much of the good intention of creating a modern metropolis has gone away through improper planning, and the quest for expediency and economy. It is a city that started well but in the headlong pursuit of progress, got a bit lost along the way. It had its genesis in 1782 in the sheltering crook of the Chao Phraya River. Royal engineers sliced a crescent canal across the neck of an oxbow to turn the lobe into an island on which a walled royal city could be built. This royal city is the crown jewel of Bangkok, encompassing its most beautiful architecture, an ethereal realm carved from gold and glitter to frame the most revered pillars of Thailand: Buddhism and the monarchy. Wat Phra Kaew (Temple of the Emerald Buddha) and the Grand Palace are the emblems of the city, their portraits identifying Bangkok in a way few city's momuments can. The adjacent Wat Po, sheltering the gigantic Reclining Buddha, is a famous herbal medicine school and its walls, covered in murals on everything from geology to royal rituals, for centuries served as a poor people's university where, by "reading" the paintings, they could understand a world beyond their immediate ken.

As the city grew towards the east, more concentric canals were carved across the rice fields. As in the former capital of Ayutthaya, the canals served as city streets plied by thousands of tiny sampans, their banks lined by houseboats that rose and fell with the monsoon floods. It was not until 1863 that the city acquired its first paved roads. In 1900, royalty moved to the Dusit district to the north and the nobles followed, building grand mansions. By the mid-20th century, the city had expanded far into the rice paddies to the east and into the jungles of Thonburi on the west side of the river.

A major economic boom in the late 1980s propelled Bangkok into a construction frenzy. While many of the skyscrapers were built with taste and restraint, the Thai willingness to let their imaginations run riot has left the city a potpourri of eclectic architecture seemingly designed by whim. Single buildings are conglomerations of a half dozen European architectural styles spanning two millenia. If Bangkok is the Los Angeles of the east, the newer sections are its Disneyland and, in moments of wanton exuberance, its Las Vegas as well.

With the building boom, Bangkok has become a city in transition, caught in the metamorphosis between caterpillar and butterfly. The innovations threaten to erase or bury its exotic past under boxes of concrete and glass, a preference for kitsch over classic design. Amidst the office towers and massive shopping complexes, the traffic snarls and snails through the streets. Yet, while its chaos repels, Bangkok continues to entice travellers. It is easy to suggest that its nightlife, temples, and superb food are the prime magnets but these are not enough to explain its enduring appeal. The reasons lie elsewhere. *Tosakan*'s "khon" mask provides a simile. Behind the building facades, just outside the central confines of the city lies the city's true heart. The buildings screen this world from view but penetrating the walls is as easy as strolling down a narrow lane.

In the back lanes are the markets where ordinary Thais browse and bargain for vegetables and household items. The lanes hold shops selling myriad wares and, since shophouses are open-fronted, offer a view of life in private living rooms. Wandering a back lane in Chinatown is like stepping back two centuries, where spice merchants sell slabs of cinnamon, craftsmen create lanterns and brush them with fat red characters for good luck, where a paper Mercedes-Benz is burned to send it to the ancestors, and an arm-thick incense stick over six feet tall glows to perfume a Chinese opera performance.

The city's Buddhist wats (monasteries or temples) offer both solitude and a sports arena. A late afternoon could bring a meeting with monks eager to converse, or a view of *takraw*, a game in which a wicker ball is kicked, elbowed, kneed or headed over a net in a display of breathtaking acrobatics.

The parks provide another insight into the Thai character; this time, at its relaxed best. City-centre Lumpini Park affords a telling contrast with the dynamism of the Silom Road office towers it borders. It is in the park that one meets the twin consituents of Bangkok: Chinese and Thai. As the sun is rising, Chinese perform stately *tai chi chuan* exercises and weave mysterious dances involving gleaming swords. Others meet by the lake to sing the songs of ancient China. In the afternoon, the park becomes Thai with teams playing soccer on the grass, young kite fliers tugging squares of paper aloft, and lovers paddling boats around the lake to escape the elders' watchful eyes. Throughout the park, Thais lounge on mats to dine on a variety of tasty foods prepared on the spot by vendors. It is the portrait of a dynamic entrepreneurial community unwinding amidst the roar of the bustling city.

Across the river, in the canals of Thon Buri, one rediscovers waterborne life as it was lived before the Thais chose cars over boats as their modes of transportation. Women in volcano-shaped palmleaf hats paddle sampans through coconut plantations and orchid nurseries, passing stilted wooden houses where mothers bath their babies on the verandahs and children splash in a watery playground.

Odd juxtaposition typifies most of Bangkok. Walk along a street past, in turn, a pharmacy selling both Western and Chinese herbal remedies, a noodle restaurant with roasted ducks hanging in a display case, a oily metalworking shop, a chic beauty salon, and a small goods store selling soap powder, toothpaste, and other sundries. It is these juxtapositions that make even a short stroll one of constant discovery.

What finally distinguishes Bangkok from its Asian

18 *A Lisu tribal woman from the northern hills is resplendent in her silver-studded vest and brilliantly-coloured dress and headdress. At a gathering of tribes in Chiang Rai each year, families meet old friends and display their craft and dancing skills.*

19 *Combining modern hair clips with the time-honoured patterns of her tribal dress, a Lahu woman represents the changing lifestyles of the tribal peoples. In a single generation, many have emerged from isolation in the hills to take an active role in the economy of the North.*

sisters is its ability to energize even jaded travellers. Just when one thinks one has seen everything the city has to offer and has let one's senses be dulled by repetition, Bangkok springs a surprise. More than one traveller has arrived, prepared to be overwhelmed by the city's grand monuments, and has found on returning home that the memories were of chance encounters with strangers or with unexpected beauty.

Unlike many cities which meld gradually into the rural areas, Thailand and Bangkok occupy two different planets; understanding one is no preparation for knowing the other. And while the city sets the tone and directions for the nation, it is the village which epitomises Thailand, home to the 70 per cent of the population dependent upon the land or the sea for its sustenance.

Green and orange are the primary colours of the Thai countryside with the roofs of Buddhist wats peeking through the green trees of villages set like islands in chartreuse seas of rice. This green is laced with a tracery of silver rivers and canals that water the luxuriant crops. Azure and blinding white are the hues of the seashore and the thousands of islands with crystalline sands which dot the aquamarine Gulf of Thailand and the Andaman Sea.

Its borders embrace a wide variety of ethnic and cultural influences. Little is known of the earliest inhabitants who, 5,000 years ago, appeared out of the mists to establish a thriving culture at the Northeastern area of Ban Chieng. There they created bronze utensils of remarkable sophistication, thereby enabling them to stake a claim as perhaps the world's first Bronze Age culture. Equally noteworthy was their buff pottery, each with a unique whorl design which was the hallmark of the civilization. As mysteriously as they appeared, these early inhabitants disappeared after only a few centuries.

While Mons from Burma and Khmers from Cambodia are credited with building the first towns in the Central Plains in the 7th and 8th centuries, they undoubtedly blended with indigenous hunters and gatherers who already occupied the Central Plains. Thais, who may have originated in southern China, first appeared in the 10th century, flowing southward across the low hills until by the 13th century, they had become the dominant population. The South was inhabited by Malays and Indian merchants who, from the 7th century onwards, had sailed from the sub-continent to establish trading communities at the mouths of major rivers. Today, Thailand is a patchwork of people and influences.

The bastion of "Thainess" is the Central Plains but even here there is a multiplicity of ethnic communities, products of eons-old migrations. There are Mon towns north and south of Bangkok and a large Chinese population in the capital and major cities. While in large part they have blended into the dominant populations, Vietnamese, Cambodians, Burmese, and Laotians who fled persecution in their own countries or who were brought to Thailand as war captives in the mid-19th century can still be found; vestiges of their mother cultures are evident in certain quarters of Bangkok. In the far northern hills are a half dozen colourful tribes many of which, until the Royal Family founded agricultural projects to introduce alternative crops, were slash-and-burn opium farmers. While many tribesmen have migrated to the towns and modern development has transformed many villages, the core of tribal life can still be found in communities dotting the ridgelines. Despite considerable differences in language, religion, and customs, the Akha, Lahu, Hmong, Yao, Karen, and Lisu live in harmony. Instead of vast, well-defined territories, each tribe's members live in dozens of population pockets that border or overlap with other tribes.

In many sections of the Northeast the language, customs, and cuisines are indistinguishable with those of Laos while the South is largely Muslim with strong Malay cultural overlays. The southern peninsula holds two tribal groups of its own: the Ngoh, a band of fuzzy-haired pygmies known for their prowess with blowguns, and the Chao Lay or sea gypsies who formerly foraged deserted beaches and reefs for coconuts and shellfish. Throughout their history, Thais have blended foreign art styles into a unique whole instantly recognizable as "Thai". Thus, in the rocket festival, the ancient stone temples and the cuisine of the Northeast, one can recognize Laotian and Khmer antecedents. Similarly, Laos and Burma have imprinted Northern culture and celebrations, rites and rituals, yet they stand as uniquely *Lanna* creations. In the South, the adaptation has been less pronounced and in many instances, it is difficult to distinguish southern Thai culture from that of Malaysia.

More than any other region, the Central Plains developed two cultures side by side: on the one hand, were the grand temple and palace complexes which more than anything bear the Thai creative stamp. At the same time, it created the Thai stilted houses which, for many people, are the emblem of Thainess. From the 17th century, contacts with foreigners led to the adoption of western styles which, with the passage of centuries, have come to dominate the architectural and fashion sensitivities of modern Thais. Although under siege by city influences, village culture has remained virtually unchanged. Thai farmers still live in stilted houses under which buffalo and other barnyard animals ruminate and the Buddhist temple or Muslim mosque is still the spiritual centre of village life. It is here that the true heart of Thailand beats.

Buddhism defines the character and culture of Thailand, a saffron thread that runs all aspects of daily life. Professed by 92 per cent (five per cent of the population are Muslims, most of whom inhabit the southern peninsula) of its people, Thailand's Theravada (Lesser Vehicle) Buddhism initially derived from the Mon culture of Burma around the 8th century. It was later refined by Sri Lankan monks who provided the models for the early stupas (monumental symbol of a spire as from the Buddhist

20 Buddha images may well outnumber Thailand's inhabitants, so numerous are they. The principal Buddha at top right is attended by dozens of lesser images in the nave of Wat Mahathat in Phet Buri, sixty miles south of Bangkok.

religion), whose lotus-bud spires rise above early religious sites.

Buddhism provides many of the warmer colours of Thai life. In the quiet dawn, saffron robes move through village and town streets as silent monks pad barefooted from house to house to receive alms from the Buddhist faithful. Orange tile roofs are the glowing suns hovering over villages. The glitter of gold is everywhere, flecking the tiny mirror mosaics that accent the white columns of the 29,000 wats that dot the countryside.

In the candle-lit interiors, worshippers press gold leaf squares onto "Buddha images". The images incorporate the 32 characteristics by which a Buddha may be recognized, since a new Buddha arrives to save humankind from itself every 5,000 years. Thais date their calendar from the birth of the last Buddha in 543 B.C..

The power and universality of the Buddhist monkhood is a dominant chord resonating through everyday life. Every Buddhist male becomes a monk for a period ranging from seven days to a lifetime. He dons the robes to atone for his sins and to ensure that, in the long cycle of lives towards perfection, he will return as a higher, more evolved being. As Thai Buddhism does not recognize the ordination of female monks, his act also bestows blessings on his mother and female relatives, ensuring that they, too, ultimately escape the cycle of rebirth and enter *nibban* or *nirvana*.

While the influence of the wat in city life has diminished with the passage of time, it is still paramount in the village. The chanting of ancient scriptures, the blue incense smoke swirling in the dim light and the ethereal stillness of the monastery are compelling forces in the lives of the laity. Each week on *Wan Phra*, the holy day determined by the lunar calendar, villagers carry bowls of food and rice on mats and feast with the monks. The ritual unites the community, and provides an opportunity to converse in a spiritual setting with people they might not see at other times during the week.

Thailand's history and art are essentially founded in Buddhism. Until the rise of the Ayuttahaya period, stone temples were built to honour the gods. Mortals and monarchs lived in wooden houses and palaces whose impermanence underscored the ephemeral nature of life. Just as people were on earth for only a short span of time, their homes and possessions would eventually disintegrate under the relentless assault of insects and jungle vegetation. Thus, the only remains of ancient cities are the stone or brick monuments and temples that symbolized the permanence of religious thought.

The earliest temple complex stood just north and east of Bangkok. At Nakhon Pathom and Lop Buri, Buddhist communities erected stupas as totemic symbols of their faith. With the 12th-century westward expansion of the Khmer empire from Angkor Wat into northeastern Thailand came the creation of sandstone and laterite temples of exquisite beauty, at

21 *The haunting yet serene face of a Lop Buri period Buddha image (8th-13th centuries) is conserved in Bangkok's National Museum. The Lop Buri style was inspired by the artists of Angkor Wat whose empire spread westward from present-day Cambodia and dotted Thailand's Northeast with beautiful temples.*

sites as far west as Phet Buri, Lop Buri, and Sukhothai.

When Khmer power waned in the 13th century, the Thais coalesced into a federation of kingdoms in the nort, establishing the Thai nation with its centre at Sukhothai. From a core of three Khmer temples, they built a gigantic city of monasteries and monuments influenced by Sri Lankan modes of architecture, and with satellite cities at Si Satchanalai and Kamphaeng Phet. In the far north, the brilliant *Lanna* culture was established at Chiang Mai at about the same time, with superb temples incorporating Burmese and Laotian styles of architecture.

Sukhothai survived only 150 years. Its preoccupation with Buddhism led to its decline and the emergence of a new empire at Ayutthaya, further south on the kingdom's main rivers.

Ayutthaya was a grand city of massive temples and gold-covered images and spires that inspired rapturous awe in the journals of European merchants and diplomats who began arriving early in the 17th century. Ayutthaya grew to be one of the most important cities of the Orient but its wealth attracted the envy of its neighbours.

After repeated invasions, Burmese armies breached its walls in 1767, stripping it of gold, burning and destroying most of its buildings and sending much of its population to Burma as slaves.

Once again, the Thais moved downriver, first to Thon Buri, across the river from Bangkok, and then to Bangkok itself w here it established a new capital and new dynasty in 1782. Its first king, Rama I, sought to restore the confidence of its shattered people by recreating the grandeur of Ayutthaya. The old royal city of present-day Bangkok is the result. Wat Phra Kaew is the Vatican of Bangkok, holding the Emerald Buddha, the realm's most sacred image, and much of its religious art. The Grand Palace, Wat Po, and Wat Arun on the opposite river bank, are the landmark monuments to which pious Thais everywhere direct their fervour.

Buddhism also serves as the inspirational fount for artists. Most of the sculpture comprises Buddha images crafted in wood, stone, or bronze in a variety of styles. The inner walls of nearly every temple are clad in colourful murals depicting the last ten incarnations (there were 550) of the man who eventually reached enlightenment and became the Buddha, as well as portrayals of major events in his life.

Today, the clamour for modern convenience has muted much of the message of Buddhism, especially in the city. Amidst the din, however, a wat is still a haven of peace from the aural and visual assaults of metropolitan life. Step off a busy street into a wat and enter an oasis of tranquillity that momentarily provides respite, where one can collect and focus one's thoughts before returning to the swirling, chaotic world outside. In the towns as well as the villages, the sense of refuge that a wat provides ensures the continuity of this age-old tradition as the principal thread binding together the lives of all Buddhist Thais.

22 *One of several golden spires flanking the Prasat Phra Thepidon at Wat Phra Kaew is supported and defended by fierce demons from Thai mythology.*

23 *In the interior of Wat Phra Kaew, the small jadeite Emerald Buddha presides over a host of images. The murals portray events in the Buddha's life and in his previous incarnations.*

24-25 *Rugged beauty abounds in Pang-nga Bay. Adjacent to Phuket island, it is renowned for its limestone monoliths rising out of the sea and towering over pristine beaches and crystalline waters.*

The Glittering City of Angels

The city with the longest name in the world is known to Thais by its shortened version: Krung Thep, City of Angels. *Meant to signify that the city is a heavenly realm, Bangkok's traffic and concrete compression suggest it is anything but ethereal. Amidst the chaos, however, rise ancient monuments and gleaming buildings which give the city its Thai stamp. Its human "angels" give it its flavour. Although hard-working,* *as the dramatic growth of their city attests, the Thais take a relaxed view of life, enjoying a quiet conversation with friends over a bowl of noodles, or a relaxing day in the park with their families. Bangkok's proximity to the countryside provides numerous opportunities to relax on a sunny beach, visit ancient sites, shop in provincial markets, float down a river, or golf at one the city's dozen courses.*

26 top In the city's core, older neighbourhoods are being bulldozed by a development frenzy that has seen the construction of more than a thousand tall buildings in the past half decade. Amid it all, however, are large population pockets, such as this one in the Makkasan area, adjacent to the Expressway, which carries on a more traditional life.

26 bottom A symbol of freedom, the Democracy Monument has been a rallying point for demonstrations against unpopular governments. It was built in Rajdamnern Avenue, the Royal Way, to commemorate the 1932 revolution which overturned 700 years of monarchic rule and gave Thailand its first constitution.

27 Wat Arun, the Temple of Dawn, rises above the Chao Phraya River opposite Wat Po, the Temple of the Reclining Buddha. Built before Bangkok's establishment as the nation's capital in 1782, it has been raised to its present height in several stages. To prevent its sinking in the soft earth, the Khmer-style stone spire rests on hundreds of huge upturned water jars.

28-29 *Friendly demons bear the enormous weight of a chedi (stupa) on their outstretched arms in the courtyard of Wat Phra Kaew. The mythical gods, originally enemies of religion, were converted to Buddhism after hearing Buddha preach. They are relatives of the 20-foot tall yaksa demons which stand guard along the inner perimeter of the complex.*

29 right *Graceful* kinnorn, *a Sanskrit word meaning "What kind of being?" are divided into* kinnara *(male) and* kinnaree *(female) and are said to inhabit the caves of the Himaphan forest in the foothills of Mount Krailas, the abode of the gods.*

30 top *The* kroot *is the Thai form of the* garuda, *the bird-like creature which transports the Hindu god Vishnu on its back. Thai kings of the present dynasty are titled "Rama", an incarnation of Vishnu, and the* kroot *appears as a symbol of royal power. Its presence on commercial buildings indicates that the company operates by royal appointment.*

30 middle left *A* yaksa *or demon giant converted to Buddhism stands guard at the door to Wat Phra Kaew, barring the entry of evil spirits.*

30 middle right *Thai chapel gables are often the canvases for Thai artistic exuberance. This one, covered in coloured mosaic tiles and gold leafed-stucco, is presided over by a praying deity.*

30 bottom *Surmounting the roofs of Thai temples the bird-like* chorfah, *often translated as "sky tassels", mark a bond between heaven and earth. Along the gable edges slither the sinuous* naga, *celestial serpents associated with water.*

30-31 *The oldest building in the Grand Palace, the Dusit Maha Prasad, is considered the purest example of Thai architecture. Once used as a royal audience chamber, it now serves as the final resting place for deceased monarchs before their cremations.*

32 *The jadeite Emerald Buddha was placed in the royal chapel of Wat Phra Kaew in 1782 after the first king of the Chakri dynasty, King Rama I, led an army to victory against the king of Laos. The image, which had led a turbulent life as a prized captive in several royal cities, was taken in triumph to Bangkok where it has since resided, revered as the holiest image in the kingdom. At the onset of the three Thai seasons - cold, hot, and rainy - its robes are changed to the appropriate garb, in a solemn ceremony presided over by King Bhumibol.*

33 right *Another mythical* kinnara, *male "what kind of being?", glitters in Wat Phra Kaew.*

33 bottom left *The spires of Wat Phra Kaew thrust skyward. The golden chedi, the Phra Si Ratana Chedi in the foreground was built as a replica of an Ayutthayan stupa. Just beyond it is the delicately-spired Library, erected to hold the Tripitaka, the holiest of Buddhist scriptures. The farthest of the three, the Prasat Phra Thepidon, is the royal pantheon.*

33 bottom right *Thailand abounds in chedis which honour the Buddha. Derived from an ancient Hindu custom of creating a mound of earth and burying religious artifacts in it, chedis were meant to remind the faithful of the Buddha's teachings. Over time, the mounds evolved into elaborate spires such as this one in Wat Phra Kaew.*

The Old
Royal City

34-35 *Bangkok was born from the fires which destroyed Ayutthaya in 1767. From the ascension of the first Chakri monarch, King Rama I, in 1782, Thailand was assailed by the Burmese from the west, the Laotians from the northeast, and the Vietnamese from the east. To protect the island city, prisoners of war were employed to dig canals as defensive moats around it. Along the eastern perimeter, a wall was erected with 14 watchtowers, only two of which remain today. This watchtower is at Pan Fah; the defensive canal lies just to the left of it. In the background is the Golden Mount, erected on a manmade hill similar to a chedi in Ayutthaya. The Mount has served as a lookout point, and in World War II, was fitted with sirens to warn of air attacks, a raucous contrast to the solemn bronze bells which normally toll the dawn.*

35 right *Chaos is nowhere more evident than in the city's streets, with a rush hour that runs round the clock, paralyzing all movement except that by foot.*

36-37 *The Chao Phraya River, the country's lifeline, flows from Thailand's northern borders to water the rich rice bowl of the Central Plains before dividing Bangkok into twin halves. Commerce began on its banks and moved east and west. Tall ships of a dozen nations unloaded consumer goods and took on cargoes bound for world markets. Today, it is still the principal channel for bulk cargoes like rice, sand, and cement but its role as the nation's principal highway is long gone. It empties into the Gulf of Thailand a few dozen miles below Bangkok.*

Movable Feasts

38 Nature has been bountiful in bestowing her gifts on Thailand. Its markets brim with lush fruits and vegetables, fish and shellfish of a quality and variety found in few cities. Markets stir to life hours before dawn as fresh produce arrives from the farms, bound for the city's lunch and dinner tables. With all these ingredients, it is little wonder that Thai chefs have created a cuisine that has found favour throughout the world.

39 It is said that every Thai is a four-star chef and that anything that can hold a stove qualifies as a restaurant. While Bangkok boasts chefs capable of preparing the world's cuisines, it is in its backstreets and hidden corners that one finds some of its most delicious dishes. Tiny sampans with charcoal stoves are paddled into canals to cook and serve noodles on the diner's doorstep. Twin baskets dangle from a shoulder poles as a woman trundles through the streets with her travelling restaurant. The baskets hold sweets and entire meals as well as stools on which patrons can squat while enjoying their feast.

Diversions

40 top *Night-time brings its own entertainments. The best known are those associated with bars inhabited by bikini-clad women who gyrate to rock tunes for the amusement of customers.*

40 bottom *More common are the myriad restaurants serving a wealth of cuisines, where atmosphere is as important as the meals served. This one thrives on its riverside location and the seafood dishes it prepares for patrons of all nationalities.*

41 top Thai boxing originated on ancient battlefields and only recently evolved into a pugilistic art. Combatants employ a lethal array of weapons - feet, knees, elbows, and fists - to encourage an opponent to retire. Boxers who fail to make the grade often take up international-style boxing.

41 bottom More clowning that combat, this form of Thai-style boxing is frowned upon by purists but it provides entertainment to diners at a major outdoor restaurant.

Quiet corners

42-43 *Like islands of serenity in the maelstrom of the city, Buddhist monasteries serve as spiritual anchors for millions of Thais. Wat Rajnadda on the right with the Golden Mount as a backdrop, is typical of the old-style wats, many of which pre-date the city's founding. In the left foreground is a recently-constructed pavilion where special foreign guests are received.*

43 right *Wat Benjamabophit, the last major wat built in Bangkok, was opened in 1900. It incorporates a number of western innovations including stained glass windows and the Carrara marble that clads its outer walls and gives it its other name: the Marble Wat.*

44-45 One of Thailand's most colourful rites is the annual Trooping of the Colours, staged each December 3. It honours, and is presided over by, His Majesty the King as part of his birthday celebrations on December 5. In the late afternoon sun, officers of elite army units gather at the royal Plaza before the old Parliament Building. Clad in their regimental colours, they march past the royal pavilion and then stand at attention as they are reviewed by Their Majesties.

46-47 Born in 1927 in Boston, Massachusetts where his father was a medical student, His Majesty King Bhumibol Adulyadej is one of the world's longest-reigning monarchs. He became king in 1946 on the death of his brother, and was crowned when he reached his majority in 1950. Although politically a figurehead ruler, he and the royal family have devoted their lives to improving conditions for rural Thais. In the 1970s, he was the first to recognize the importance of providing alternative employment for opium-growing hill tribesmen. He introduced crops and marketing techniques that have improved their lives. He soon moved into Thai villages to carry out similar projects, spending months each year tramping through farmlands, map in hand, to plot small-scale irrigation canals, and farming techniques to make the villagers better farmers. Queen Sirikit has endeavoured to revive old crafts and provide skills and money-earning opportunities for villagers, especially women. Here, King Bhumibol lights candles at a religious observance as part of his birthday celebrations.

Silent Grace

48-49 *Thai dance-drama originated in the royal courts. Resplendent in costumes that glitter like the mosaics on temples, the dancers rely on their hands and body movements to tell the story of ancient heroes like the mythical god-king Rama and his beautiful wife Sita. The Ramakhien, which has found favour throughout Southeast Asia, travelled to Thailand from India, probably via the courts of Angkor Wat where many other Thai traditions originated. Off-stage singers, backed by musicians, supply the lyrics for the dancers whose faces never move during their performances. There are many variants of the original* lakhon *including the "khon" drama in which all the actors except three wear masks.*

Bones of a Nation

Thailand's wealth has come from the land and from people like these who have for eons tilled and cultivated it. The ancient rhyme "from the land comes rice, from the waters come fish" sums up the two principal constituents of the Thai diet, and the foundation stone of its economy.
In the North and Northeast, Thais grow a dry land, glutinous rice; in the Central Plains and South, paddy rice is planted in ponds of water. At harvest time, however, the backbreaking work of cutting, threshing and winnowing is the same for both. Rich soil fed by irrigation water allows the farmers to harvest two, and sometimes three, crops a year. Those fields watered by the clouds yield a single crop.

50-51 Agriculture employs more than 70 percent of the nation's work force. While machinery has removed some of the drudgery from rice planting, most of the work is done by hand. In the past few decades, the land has been transformed from producing a single crop, rice, to producing numerous crops in whose export Thailand now leads the world. Sweet pineapples grown primarily along the southern peninsula and the southeast have made Thailand the world's number one exporter of canned pineapples. Crops unknown 20 years ago now thrive in Thailand's rich soil. Locally-grown strawberries, asparagus, mushrooms, coffee, and others appear on dinner tables in many parts of the world, in part, the end product of a thriving agro-industry which converts raw produce into frozen or canned foods. Orchids cut from nurseries in the afternoon are jet-freighted overnight to be sold in the marketplaces of major European cities the following morning.

Northern Forests

52-53 *Teak forests built the palaces and the economy of the North. Elephants and their mahouts were the brawn of the industry, the only vehicles capable of penetrating thick jungles and climbing steep slopes to drag out the logs. Most of the vast timber stands have been felled and the forest floor converted into paddy fields to serve a growing demand for tillage land. To protect the remaining forests, the government issued a nationwide* logging ban in 1989. Today, logs are transported across the border from Burma on trucks. Elephants are still trained at schools in Lampang and north of Chiang Mai but the enormous beasts no longer work in the forests. Instead, they demonstrate their skills in tourist shows and carry foreign travellers on bumpy journeys through the hills.

54-55 *Geographically, the Golden Triangle describes the point where the* borders of Thailand, Burma and Laos conjoin. But in recent years, the name has gained the more sinister connotation of heroin production and warlord caravans (persons transporting opium or heroin), although in the Thai portion of the Triangle, the principal contraband is tourist trinkets. The Triangle's apex is this small region where the Mekong River and its tributaries mark the boundaries of the three countries.

Flowers of Evil

56 *A large portion of the world's opium was once grown in the hills of the Golden Triangle and processed into heroin across the border in Burma. Several of Thailand's hilltribes were proficient in cultivating the deadly crop but their income from it was minimal and they lived in dire poverty, many of them addicted to the noxious fumes.*

In the early 1970s, they became the focus of a royal programme to provide them with a more lucrative means of earning a living, thereby weaning them away from the clutches of the opium smugglers. For the majority of the tribes, the programme has brought new prosperity and enhanced futures for their children.

57 *While not all the stands of opium have been eradicated due to the ease with which it can be concealed in isolated valleys far beyond the vigilance of patrolling police, the trade has been severely curtailed. Today, gardens of poppies are grown for the beauty of their flowers. The* bulbs are dried and sold to foreigners as exotic floral decorations. To earn their living, tribesmen and women apply their cultivation skills to growing more profitable flowers like chrysanthemums which are trucked to the larger cities for sale in the markets or are dried and exported.*

58-59 *Karen tribal women gather flowers for sale in the towns. While most tribes are animist, many Karens several decades ago converted to Christianity. Rather than living in separate nations, the half dozen major tribes of the North live in population pockets surrounded by other tribes. Thus, in a single day one may walk through a Karen, a Yao, Hmong, and Lisu village and then repeat the sequence the following day. Despite speaking different, mutually incomprehensible languages, and following different customs, the tribes are remarkable for living in harmony with each other.*

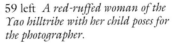

59 left *A red-ruffed woman of the Yao hilltribe with her child poses for the photographer.*

59 right *Living along the border with Burma are the Pawdawn group of the Karen tribe. Their women are known for the brass rings that encircle their necks. Although called the "Long-necked Karens", the rings do not stretch the necks but depress the collarbones. The practice is rapidly disappearing, discarded as a relic of outmoded fashion.*

60-61 *Hmong women, often called Meo, are noted for the bright colours of their costumes. Their artisans are famed for their silver craftsmanship which is employed in the creation of beautiful necklaces and other decorative jewellery.*
Their costumes display a legacy of British colonialism in India and Burma with silver coins of the British Raj incorporated into the headdress.

62-63 *Yao men and women gather for ceremonial dances in the early morning. The flirtatious dances are meant to pair the youths for possible courtship and later marriage. Despite the invasion of modern values, the old customs and lore still hold much of their former power.*

64-65 *The terraced fields of the North are watered by an intricate irrigation system seven centuries old that utilizes the waters of small streams to ensure healthy plants in often rugged terrain. Today, agriculture is expanding, with new vegetable crops harvested and transported to distant markets in a day.*

66 top *In May as the sun is still searing the sky, rice seed beds are planted. When the rains fall in early June, the arduous task of transplanting begins. The tender shoots are removed from the seedbeds and hand planted, one by one, in fields turned to muck by the rains.*

66 bottom *Buffalo, the traditional beasts of burden, are becoming a rare sight in Thailand as "iron buffalo" rototillers churn the ground to prepare the fields for planting.*

67 *From the air, the village with its school, wat, and compound of stupas, sits like an island amid the dry fields of the late April hot season. When the rains fall, these fields will become lush seas of green rice.*

New Crops

68-69 *Northern valleys formerly blanketed in trees, and later in rice, are now covered in cabbages, lettuce and other crops introduced only two decades ago to provide tribesmen with a new source of income.*

70-71 *The grey skies of the early monsoon season unleash torrents of rain which the parched ground soaks up. This is the signal for farmers to begin transplanting rice from the seedbeds to individual fields surrounded by low earthen walls which capture the water. The transplanting, a backbreaking task, has given rise to an axiom describing the farmer's lot: "Face to the ground and back to the sky. Forever." In many areas, hardy trees whose roots do not drown stand in the same fields.*

72-73 *Taking a break at harvest time in the North, two women light up hand-rolled cheroots filled with Northern tobacco. Although the North produces a Virginia variety regarded as one of the smoothest in the world, village men and women prefer their home-grown harsh strain.*

Dressed for the Gods

74 *The stellar event in a boy's life is his
ordination into the Buddhist monkhood.
In Mae Hong Son, inhabited by Shan
(also called Thai Yai) people who are
culturally and linguistically akin to the
Thais, the Poy Sang Long (called* Buat
Luk Kaew *or "ordaining a precious son"
in Thai) ceremony has a different flavour.
Dressed in pastel costumes, young boys are
borne to the temple on elephants or on the
shoulders of friends and relatives.*

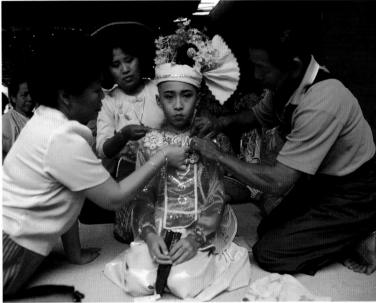

75 left *The somber pastel colours of the Burmese-inspired Poy Sang Long ceremony are a marked contrast to the white robes assumed by a Buddhist novice in other parts of Thailand.*

75 right *Parents play an important role in the Poy Sang Long rite as it is to make merit for them that their child is ordained into the priesthood. The boy is generally nine years old, an age at which he is considered uncorrupted by the world.*

76-77 *Costumed and bejewelled boys eat before setting off for the ordination ceremony. As the ordination occurs on only one day in April, many boys are ordained together and the event becomes a community celebration.*

Battle of the Beasts

78-79 *In ancient wars, elephants were the tank corps of Southeast-Asian battles. A royal commander directed his army's movements from the vantage point of a howdah, high on an elephant's back, while foot soldiers guarded each of the beast's four legs. In rare instances, the outcome of an encounter was determined by combat between the opposing monarchs wielding an arsenal of lances, spears and tridents.*

There are numerous stories of bravery in elephant wars. In a 15th-century battle with the Burmese, King Naresuan was locked in a duel to the death with a Burmese prince. Seeing her husband in a disadvantageous position, Queen Suriyothai spurred her elephant between the pair and took the lance blow intended for her spouse. A chedi honouring her stands in the old city of Ayutthaya. Each year at the Elephant Round-up in the northeastern town of Surin, the ancient battles are re-enacted by dozens of elephants and hundreds of soldiers.

80-81 *Throughout Thai history, rivers have been the highways into the countryside, and canals the streets of the towns.*
Today, despite the dominance of cars and trucks, villagers prefer to paddle their boats to market, carrying produce they have risen hours before

dawn to harvest. In the market, they sell their goods to other vendors or to merchants from town markets.
So brisk is the business that by 9 a.m., most vendors are already paddling back home with the day's earnings and the few goods they have purchased for household use.

82-83 *Each morning, monks walk through villages with their alms bowls which are filled with rice and curries by the faithful. In regions cut by many streams, the monks paddle small sampans through the canals, stopping at houses to receive their daily meal which they share with older monks.*

Coloured disks

84-85 *The* Lanna *culture of the North arose independently of that of the Central Plains so that its creations and styles are distinct from those of its southern neighbours. Among the most renowned of Chiang Mai arts is umbrella-making. In the village of Borsang, east of the city, the umbrella skeletons are crafted from bamboo. The struts are bound together with threads to create the umbrella's frame. The bark of* the sah *tree is soaked and laid out in sheets to dry in the sun. Then, this* sah *paper is applied as the skin of the umbrella. Although the paper fabric is delicate, it becomes impervious to rain once it has been lacquered. The most popular treatment, however, is to paint the umbrella surface in bright nature motifs. The umbrellas range in size from tiny sun parasols to garden umbrellas nine feet in diameter.*

86-87 *When the cool air of winter (December-February) brings northern flowers to their brightest bloom, Chiang Mai blossoms. A celebration of nature's beauty, the annual flower festival, offers exhibitions of the best of the town's gardens. The highlight is a grand procession with floral floats and beauty queens parading through the streets. Thousands of flowers are utilized in creating the ephemeral beauty that will die in a day, an object lesson in the transitoriness of life that Buddhism extols.*

88-89 *When the sun is at its burning brightest on April 13, Thais cool off by celebrating* Songkran. *Formerly, the festival marked the end of one year and the beginning of the next. Decades ago, the new year was shifted to January 1 to accord with world standards but* Songkran *still has religious significance. On April 12, the city's principal Buddha image is drawn in a procession through the streets. Worshippers splash water on it to cleanse it and to earn merit. The following day, all thoughts of solemnity are forgotten. In the past, celebrants sprinkled water on friends and relatives to cleanse them of the old year's sins and bestow blessings on them for the coming year. That, in principal, is still how the festival is celebrated but as the day heats up, all thoughts of moderation are discarded. What begins as droplets of water sprinkled on passersby, becomes torrents of water shot from hoses. Everyone is fair game and even monks are drenched. In Chiang Mai, it is celebrated with particular gusto and is highlighted by a parade through the streets.*

Crystalline
Colours

90-91 *Pang-nga Bay is one of the natural wonders of Asia. Bordered on the west by the island of Phuket, the bay is dozens of miles wide, and filled with limestone monoliths rising hundreds of feet out of the Andaman Sea. Trees cling to vertical slopes of pinnacles that, in the early morning, loom out of the mists like tall ships. Many of the limestone mountains are punctuated by caves leading to open-roofed lagoons*

inhabited by families of monkeys stranded there by rising seas eons ago. Along the rims of the bay are mangrove forests with lungfish walking across the mud flats. On some islands, Muslim fishing villages perch on stilts high above the waves. The area was once the haunt of smugglers and pirates whose graceful old junks now convey cargoes of travellers on journeys into this incredible world.

Beaches and Bays

92 *Phuket's beauty lies in its dozens of coves sculpted from the green hills and fringed by snow-white, powdery sands. Each bay has a distinct personality, some with waves that crash on sands that squeak; others with long, low rollers that break gently on long sloping beaches.*

93 *Karon Bay, with its warm aquamarine waters, is typical of the beaches along Phuket's sundown shore.*

94-95 *Phi Phi Don, at the southern end of Pang-nga Bay, is one of Asia's most beautiful islands. A narrow strand of palm-covered beach links two groups of magnificent limestone mountains at the southern extremity of Pang-nga Bay. The coral reefs are inhabited by schools of brightly-coloured tropical fish and the sheltered bay is a popular anchorage for long-distance yachts.*

96-97 *Pattaya, the first of Thailand's beaches to be developed for tourism, is regarded as one of Asia's best beach resorts for its accommodation and facilities. Its broad crescent bay is studded with dozens of tall hotels and the sports and recreation opportunities it offers can keep even the most restless visitor active. While the impact of tourism has been severe, it is still possible to find quiet corners of superb beauty and serenity.*

Homage in Gold

Gold, orange, and earth browns are the colours of Buddhist Thailand, hues seen in village and city alike. The warm browns glow in the laterite and sandstone of Sukhothai's ancient monuments and in the Khmer temples of the Northeast. It also illumines the wooden temples of the North. Because Thailand's mountains yield little good construction stone, Central Plains architects turned to the earth, gouging out the clay in which their crops flourished and baking it into deep orange bricks which they stacked into the great palaces and temples of Ayutthaya. Since ancient times, orange has been the colour of monk's robes and temple roofs, and gold adorns everything regarded as sacred.

98 top Two shades of orange tiles framed in green are the hues of temple roofs, rectangles of colour among the trees that even from great distance signify the presence of a town in the forest. On royal wats, the central roof colour is deep blue with an orange border as is seen here at Wat Pra Kaew, the temple of the Emerald Buddha.

98 bottom The roofs of monks' quarters sit amidst the roofs of one of Bangkok's oldest temples, Wat Saket at the base of the Golden Mount.

99 This exquisite pavilion at the former summer palace at Bang Pa-in near Ayutthaya is considered a masterpiece of Thai architecture. It was the model for a similar pavilion erected at the Brussels World Fair in 1957.

100 left *The Phra Buddha Jinarat, a 14th-century image in the Sukhothai style, is considered one of the most beautiful in Thai Buddhism. It occupies the central nave of Wat Mahathat in the northern city of Phitsanuloke and is said to have wept blood when the town was defeated by the armies of Ayutthaya the same century.*

100-101 *The design of Wat Mahathat, the most important monastery complex in Sukhothai, was inspired by Sri Lankan wats. Thailand had acquired its Buddhism in the 7th and 8th centuries from India but the country's isolation from the Indian founts of Buddhism had resulted in a corruption of its tenets and the texts. In the 14th century, Thai Buddhists adopted the Theravada or Lesser Vehicle form of the religion as did Sri Lanka, which became an important religious centre. Thai monks sailed to Sri Lanka to obtain more accurate scriptures and Sri Lankan monks were invited to preach in Sukhothai. They came with architects who introduced the concept of the lotus bud finial on chedis, a spire treatment also seen in nearby Si Satchanalai.*

102-103 *The delicate architecture of Sukhothai suggests a kingdom preoccupied with ethereal matters, a predilection for religion which ultimately led to the city's decline as a major power. Ayutthaya, which succeeded it, was an empire builder which, while devoutly Buddhist, focussed on earthly matters. Its architecture reflects this attitude. Its monuments are muscular, a statement of human endeavour and pride. They trumpet the achievements of an important kingdom expanding its realm through conquest and economic growth. Wat Rajburana is one of many Ayutthayan monuments which embody this philosophy.*

104-105 *The delicacy of columns and spires in Sukhothai, and of contemplative beauty of the reflecting ponds is evident in this depiction of Wat Mahathat.*

106 *Although a Buddha image is meant to remind devout Buddhists of the Teacher's doctrine, it is easy for the foreigner who is watching Thais lavish attention on it with incense sticks, flowers, candles and gold leaf, to think that it is the image itself which is being worshipped. For rural Thais, the distinction between the two is hazy. For monks, it is more clearly defined as with this monk praying at the feet of a gigantic image in the courtyard of Bangkok's Wat In.*

107 top *Many young boys, orphans or too poor to be supported by their families, become* nag *or novices, a means of enabling society to provide for their needs. When in their teens, they may opt to be ordained as fully-fledged monks.*

107 bottom *Monks rise at dawn to walk the streets collecting alms and food from pious Buddhists waiting outside their homes. The food is carried back to the wat to be shared with all, the only meal the monks will eat all day. On Wan Phra, the weekly Buddhist holy day, the faithful take the food to the monasteries to eat and talk with the monks. The meal must be consumed before noon.*

108-109 *The large orange-roofed chapel, Viharn Phra Mongkon Bopit, shelters Ayutthaya's largest seated bronze Buddha image. The original building was torched by Burmese invaders in 1767 and for years, until a new chapel was built in 1951, it sat in the sun.*

109 top *Buddha images abound in Ayutthaya. While those in the chapels are normally cast of bronze, these and their attendants in the former cloisters of Wat Yai Monkol, are made of stucco-covered brick.*

109 bottom *The triple chedis (stupas) of Wat Phra Si Sanphet are Ayutthaya's best-known symbols. They stand immediately behind Viharn Phra Mongkon Bopit, sandwiched between it and the old palace. Each holds the ashes of a 16th-century king and may have been part of an old royal temple.*

110-111 *Thai classical dancers in their gilded headdresses, make an offering of fragrant garlands, incense and candles to a bronze Buddha image.*

112 *Si Satchanalai, on the banks of the Yom River, was subordinate to the power of the Sukhothai king and protected the realm's northern flanks. Like Sukhothai, its architecture is inspired by Sri Lankan models with their delicate, tapering spires. Wat Chang Lom displays an architectural feature found in several other Sukhothai and Chiang Mai stupas: elephant caryatids seemingly supporting the structure on their backs and giving the stupa its name, "encircled by elephants". Elephants appear frequently as Buddhist symbols. It is said that Buddha's mother conceived him when a white elephant touched his trunk to her side during a dream.*

113 *Chamathewi was a seventh century princess of Lop Buri, an ancient central Thai kingdom. Seeking to expand her realm, she travelled north to establish the city of Lamphun, a few dozen miles south of Chiang Mai. Its most notable monument is the temple named after her, Wat Chamathewi. The pyramidal structure, called a* wat chedi sii liem, *or "four-sided stupa" is characterized by tiers of niches, each alcove holding a Buddha image. Chedis of the same design are found in several northern cities including Chiang Mai.*

Echoes of Angkor

114 *Phimai, near the present-day town of Nakhon Ratchasima, was the final stop on a pilgrimage route from Angkor Wat marked by 112 resthouses. The old town with its sandstone Khmer-style towers dates from the latter half of the 12th century before the Angkorian kings converted from Hinduism to Buddhism. Thus the figures depicted are those from the Hindu pantheon of deities.*

115 *Some of the same Angkorian influences can be seen in temples like Wat Phra Phai Luang in Sukhothai. Before it became the capital of the new Thai nation in the 13th century, Sukhothai was an outpost of the Angkorian empire.*
Its original three shrines were built by Khmer architects many of whose motifs can be found in later Thai structures.

116-117 *Two young men, their heads shaven and wearing the white robes of novices, have just been examined by the abbot of a wat and found worthy of ordination into the Buddhist monkhood.*
Having received their new orange robes, they pray and make offerings of thanksgiving before donning their garb and taking up residence in the monastery.

118-119 *In recognition of the importance of parents, the mother of a young Buddhist novice is the first to snip a lock of hair from her son's head. Her participation is important as it is partially to make merit for her and other female relatives that the young man enters the monkhood, since there are no provisions for the ordination of nuns. Monks then shave the boy's skull and eyebrows, after which his mother, aided by her husband, pours water over her son's head to wash away the shaved hair and, with it, any sins her son might have committed in the past. Buddhist tradition requires that a man enter the monkhood once in his life for a period of seven or more days. Companies grant male employees leave with pay during their stay in the monastery.*

119 right *Topknot cutting was once a common ceremony among royal and noble children. Today, it has lapsed in popularity, the rite depicted here for a young girl being a rare instance. The ceremony marks the child's ascension to puberty. It is presided over by a Brahman priest as it is a lay rather than a religious ceremony although Buddhist monks are in attendance. The tradition of Brahman priests presiding over royal state ceremonies and rites of passage derives from the Cambodian courts of Angkor which Thai armies conquered in the 15th century and from which they brought the Brahman priests. Today, the priests have their own temple near Bangkok's Wat Suthat.*

120 *Mae Hong Son, on the border with Burma in the far northwest, was once considered Thailand's Siberia where erring officials were sent as punishment. It was regarded as a cold, foggy valley, filled with strange cultures, and far removed from the bustle of the city. Today, these qualities are among the prime reasons for its popularity. Its Burmese-style architecture is another key attraction. Crowing a tall hill, the gleaming white chedis of Wat Doi Kong Mu stand sentinel above the valley in which the town nestles.*

121 *On the valley floor is a lake and reflected in it are the golden spires of another jewel-like Burmese temple, Wat Jong Klang.*

122 *Contrary to popular Western thought, Buddha images are not intended as representations of a real person. They incorporate the 32* raksanas *or characteristics by which the Lord Buddha may be recognized. Devised eons ago, they are vitally important as new Buddhas appear at set intervals throughout history and the* raksana *indicate their divinity to the faithful. The cycle begins with the arrival of a new Buddha and then, like a rainbow, humankind progresses to an apex after 2,500 years before it begins its descent and a new Buddha must be born to save civilization from itself. The last Buddha was born in 543 B.C. meaning that 1957 was the apogee. The next Buddha, the Maitreya, will appear in 4457 A.D. As in the past, he will be recognized by his* raksanas *which include wedge-shaped heels, fingers of equal length, bow-shaped eyebrows and, oddly, blue eyes. The image's ear lobes, distended by heavy gold earrings, recall the Buddha's life as a prince before he left his palace at age 30 to seek enlightenment.*

123 left *Mythical animals abound in Thai art. In Buddhist temples, they add an animistic note to the solemnity of the other architecture. The* naga *is a dragon-like beast associated with water and despite its playful appearance it commands great power. Pairs of* nagas *slither down stairway balustrades and along gables, their elaborately-decorated bodies ending in horned and goateed heads. They are the presiding deities at the annual* Songkran *festival, propitiated for their magical power to bring rain during the subsequent monsoon season.*

123 right *The* dvarapala *or temple door guardians come in many forms but their duty is the same: to protect the chapel's inner sanctum from evil spirits.*

124-125 *Contrasting styles in* Lanna *architecture are evident in two of its most famous temples, Wat Suan Dok, below, and Wat Doi Suthep, opposite page. Wat Suan Dok is associated with the monk Summa who discovered an important relic which subsequently broke into two pieces. One half was kept at Wat Suan Dok. The other half was placed on the back of a wandering elephant; wherever it halted for the night, a temple would be built. The beast climbed the tall hill overlooking Chiang Mai and there, like a tiny crown, Wat Phra That Doi Suthep, was built. Its gleaming chedi and filigree brass umbrellas are the most photographed sights in the North.*

126-127 *Wat Si Chum, one of Sukhothai's best known wats, is little more than a roofless brick and stucco box but it protects an enormous seated Buddha image.*
Before an important battle, the image is said to have spoken to Thai soldiers, inspiring them to valour and victory. Had they known that there is a stairway concealed in the surrounding wall and that it leads to a small window just behind the image, they might have located a less ethereal source for the divine voice.
A young monk applies gold leaf to a hand twice as tall as he, an act of veneration for this seven centuries old image.

128 *Wat Sriket in Chiang Rai holds a solemn, majestic gilt Buddha.*

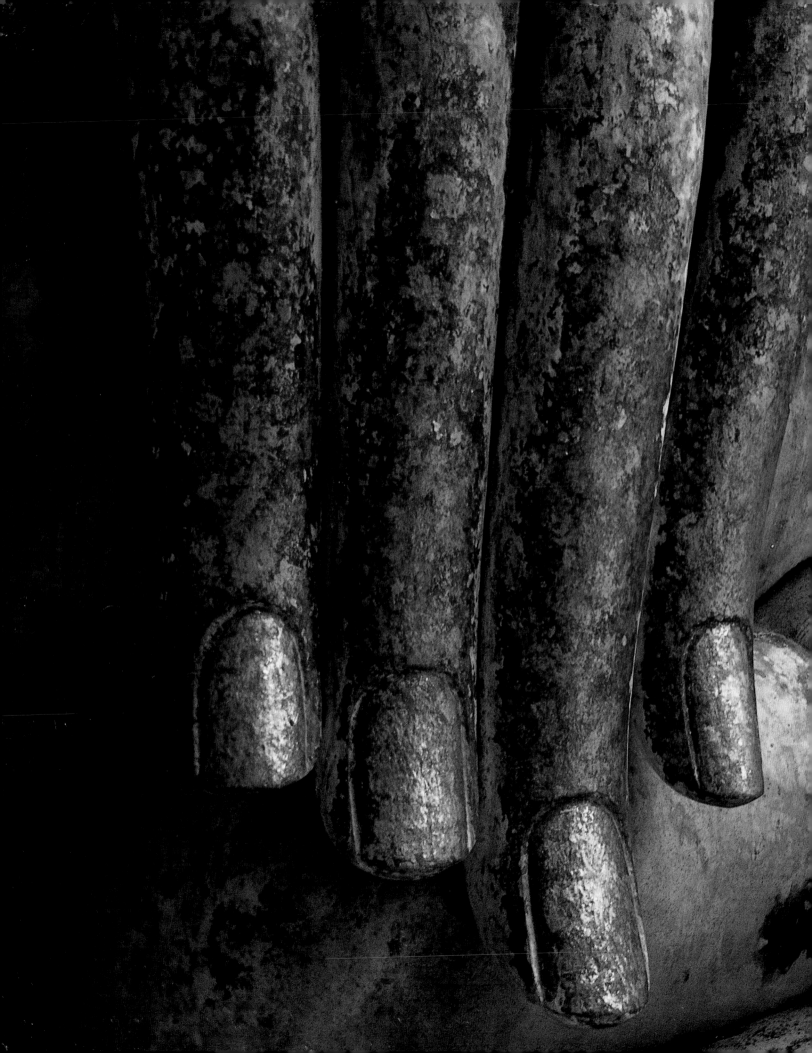

Photo Credits:

Marcello Bertinetti / Archivio White Star:
Pages 9, 30, 33, 98 top.

S. T. Amerasinghe / Apa Photo Agency:
Page 22.

Apa Photo Agency:
Pages 26, 29.

J. Beck / Apa Photo Agency:
Pages 43, 106.

Cristiana Carvalho / Apa Photo Agecny:
Page 61.

Jean Léo Dugast / Apa Photo Agency:
pages 4-5, 24-25, 35, 50 bottom, 51, 72-73, 80, 116-117, 118, 119, 126-127.

Alain Evrard / Apa Photo Agency:
Pages 1, 16, 18, 19, 40, 46-47, 58, 59, 64-65, 68, 69, 74, 75, 76-77, 86, 88, 89 bottom, 107, 121, 122, 128.

Ghirotti / SIE:
Page 84.

J. Gocher / Apa Photo Agency:
Page 10-11.

Manfred Gottschalk / Apa Photo Agency:
Pages 90, 109 bottom.

A. Greensmith / Ardea London:
Page 56.

Dallas & John Heaton / Apa Photo Agency:
Cover, pages 27, 53, 66 bottom, 96, 99.

Robert Knight / Apa Photo Agency:
Page 28-29.

Rainer Krack / Apa Photo Agency:
Page 45 top.

Robert McLeod / Apa Photo Agency:
Page 89 top.

Philippe Montbazet / Explorer:
Page 57.

Ben Nakayama / Apa Photo Agency:
Page 109 top.

R.C.A. Nichols / Apa Photo Agency:
Back cover, page 94-95.

G.P. Reichell / Apa Photo Agency:
Page 38 left.

Philippe Roy / Explorer:
Page 54-55.

David Ryan / Apa Photo Agency:
Pages 78, 79.

Rick Strange / Apa Photo Agency:
Pages 6, 14-15, 97, 101, 112, 125.

Luca Invernizzi Tettoni / Apa Photo Agency:
Pages 2-3, 7, 12-13, 17 bottom, 20, 21, 23, 31, 32, 34, 36-37, 38 right, 39, 41 bottom, 42, 44, 49, 50 top, 52, 60, 62-63, 66 top, 67, 70-71, 82-83, 85, 87, 91, 92, 93, 98 bottom, 100, 102-103, 104-105, 108, 110-111, 113, 114, 115, 120, 123 left, 124.

Bill Wassman / Apa Photo Agency:
Pages 17 top, 41 top, 45 bottom, 48, 123 right.

W. M. Waterfall / Apa Photo Agency:
Page 81.